PICTURE F.

SPACECRAFT

MW01178383

PICTURE FACTS

SPACECRAFT

N. S. Barrett

Franklin Watts

London   New York   Sydney   Toronto

Published by:

Franklin Watts
96 Leonard Street
London EC2A 4RH

Franklin Watts Australia
14 Mars Road
Lane Cove
NSW 2066

ISBN: Paperback edition 0 7496 0649 5
          Hardback edition: 0 86313 281 2

Copyright © 1985 Franklin Watts

Paperback edition 1991

Hardback edition published
in the Picture Library series.

Printed in Singapore

Designed by
Barrett & Willard

Photographs by
NASA
Novosti
European Space Agency
Spacecharts/JPL

Illustration by
Janos Marffy

Technical Consultant
Robin Kerrod

Contents

Introduction

Hundreds of spacecraft circle the Earth. Some spacecraft go to the Moon and the planets. They carry special cameras and other equipment to send back information to Earth.

Manned spacecraft have landed astronauts on the Moon. In the US programme, Space Shuttle orbiters take people and whole laboratories into space.

△ The Space Shuttle lifts off. The rocket boosters and large fuel tank are discarded on each Shuttle mission. Unmanned spacecraft, mainly satellites, are launched from the Shuttle.

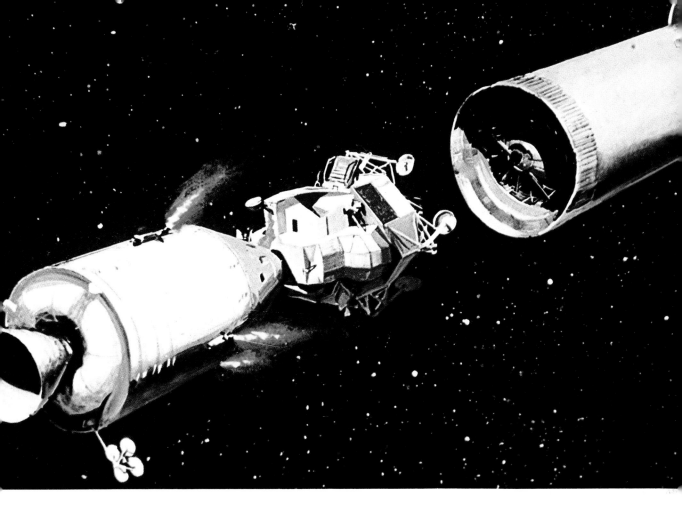

Unmanned spacecraft are either satellites or probes.

There are many kinds of unmanned satellites. They are used for such work as carrying TV signals or gathering weather information.

Space probes are used to explore other worlds. Some land on the Moon or planets. They even travel beyond our Solar System.

△ The picture shows how Apollo 11 separated from the Saturn rocket on its way to land the first men on the Moon. The Lunar Module, the spacecraft that landed on the Moon, is to the right of the jets.

The spacecraft

The Space Shuttle is a versatile spacecraft. It can take up all kinds of satellites and other spacecraft in its cargo, or payload, bay. The payload shown here is Spacelab, designed and built for NASA by the European Space Agency. Up to four people can perform scientific tests in this orbiting laboratory. Spacelab and its pallets remain inside the orbiter throughout the mission.

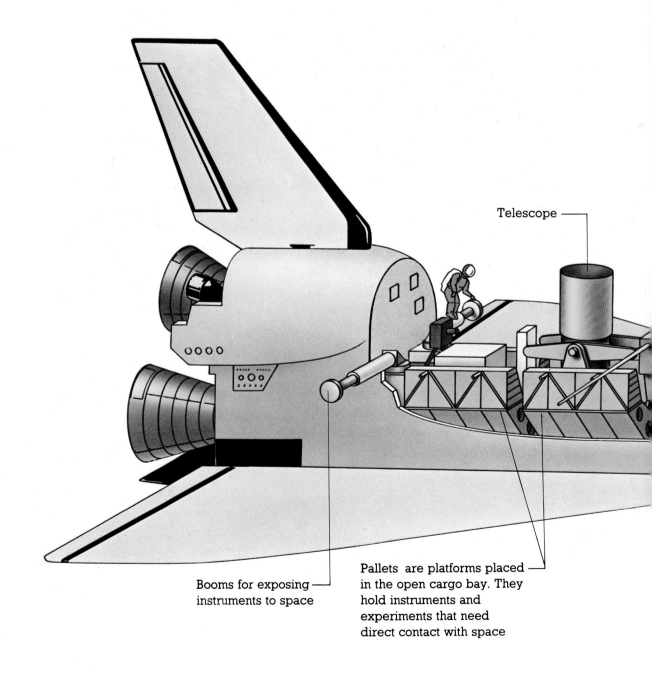

Telescope

Booms for exposing instruments to space

Pallets are platforms placed in the open cargo bay. They hold instruments and experiments that need direct contact with space

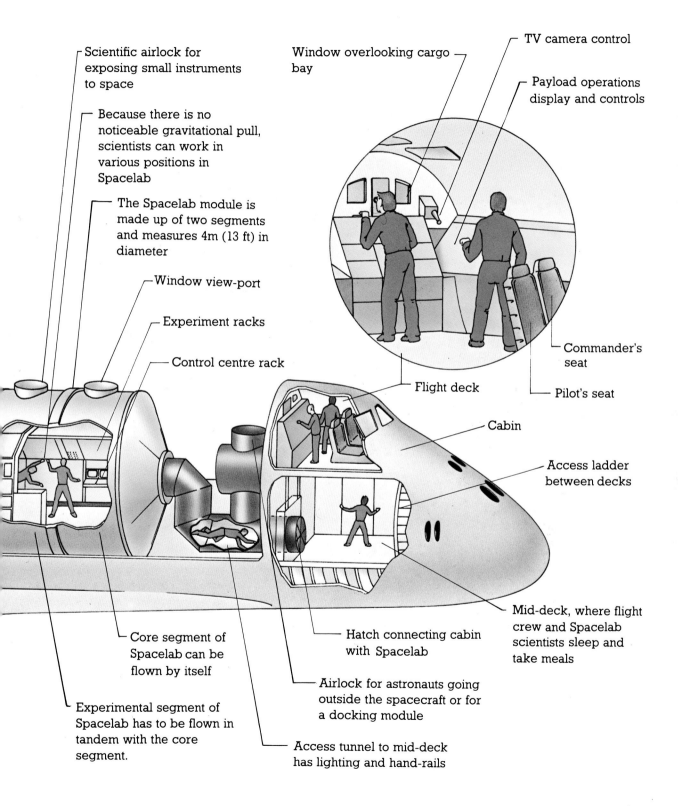

Scientific airlock for exposing small instruments to space

Because there is no noticeable gravitational pull, scientists can work in various positions in Spacelab

The Spacelab module is made up of two segments and measures 4m (13 ft) in diameter

Window view-port

Experiment racks

Control centre rack

Window overlooking cargo bay

TV camera control

Payload operations display and controls

Commander's seat

Pilot's seat

Flight deck

Cabin

Access ladder between decks

Core segment of Spacelab can be flown by itself

Experimental segment of Spacelab has to be flown in tandem with the core segment.

Hatch connecting cabin with Spacelab

Airlock for astronauts going outside the spacecraft or for a docking module

Access tunnel to mid-deck has lighting and hand-rails

Mid-deck, where flight crew and Spacelab scientists sleep and take meals

Manned spacecraft

The Space Shuttle takes people and equipment into space and is used for launching satellites into orbit around the Earth.

The spacecraft part of the Shuttle system is called the orbiter. The Shuttle fleet has four orbiters. There is plenty of room to live and work in the orbiter.

▽ Four astronauts float about in the roomy cabin of the Space Shuttle orbiter.

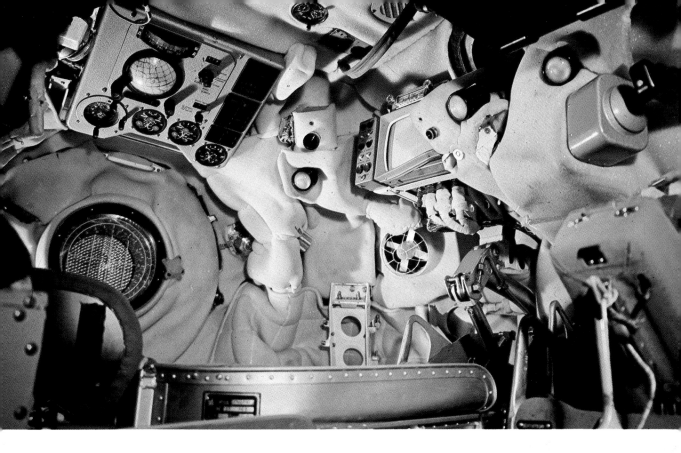

The spacecraft used for man's first steps into space had little room for the astronauts themselves. Improved rocket power was first used to increase the number of astronauts that could be carried.

△ Inside the Russian spacecraft Voskhod I. It was the first multiseater spaceship, carrying three cosmonauts.

The Russian Vostok and the US Mercury were the first one-man spacecraft. Gemini carried two astronauts. Voskhod and Apollo both carried three. The Soyuz series varied between one and three astronauts.

◁ The bell-shaped Mercury capsule was the first American manned spacecraft. There was just room for one astronaut squeezed in among all the instruments.

▽ A two-man Gemini spacecraft pictured from a second Gemini as the two became the first spacecraft to meet in space.

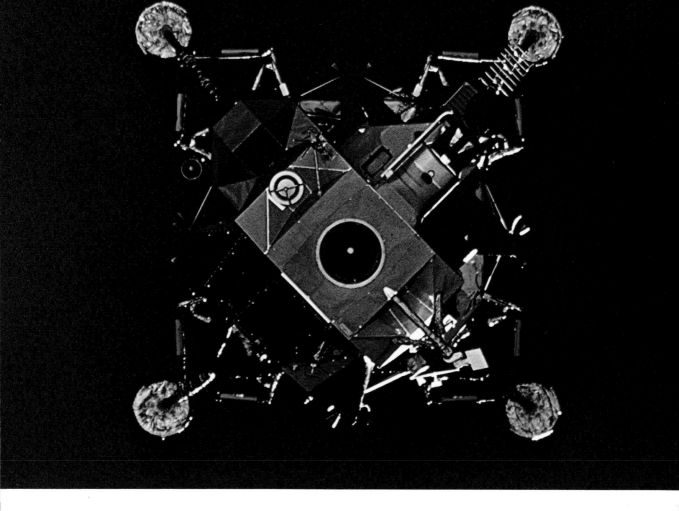

During the flights of the early manned spacecraft, astronauts learnt how to live in space. They experienced tremendous forces at the launch, and the curious effects of "weightlessness" in orbit.

Special manoeuvres were practised. Spacecraft met and joined in space. They orbited the Moon and landed on its surface.

△ The Lunar Module of an Apollo spacecraft pictured from the Command Module. On Apollo missions to the Moon, two astronauts landed on the Moon in the Lunar Module while a third orbited the Moon in the Command Module, waiting for them to return.

▷ Spacecraft on display at the Kennedy Space Center in Florida. On the ground is the Apollo Command and Service Module (CSM) which met and docked in space with the Russian spacecraft Soyuz, which is displayed hanging above it.

In this first joint mission between the two countries, American and Russian astronauts linked up in space in July 1975. The two spacecraft remained locked together for two days. The astronauts and cosmonauts visited each other's craft.

Space stations

Space stations are spacecraft that stay in orbit for long periods. Other spacecraft bring changes of crew and personnel.

The Russians have put a whole series of Salyut space stations into orbit. The first American space station was Skylab, an orbiting laboratory launched in 1973. There are plans to use the Space Shuttle to build a station as a stopping-off place for spaceships.

△ Skylab, the American space station launched into orbit in 1973. Three separate crews worked in Skylab, each with three astronauts. They studied the Sun and the Earth, and carried out experiments. After six years in orbit, Skylab re-entered the Earth's atmosphere and broke up.

▷ Astronaut Owen Garriott at work on the outside of Skylab.

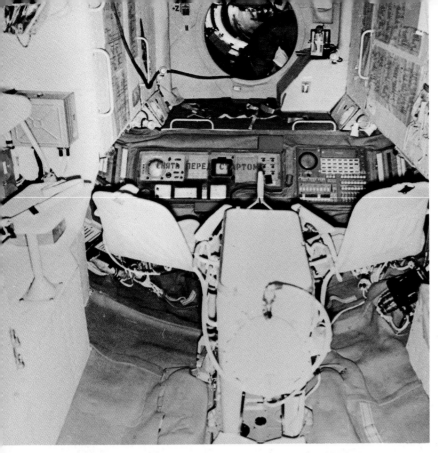

◁ Inside Salyut, the Russian space station. The picture shows the working compartment of Salyut's main section, with the control panel and seats for the crew. The hatch leads to the Soyuz spacecraft.

▽ A design for a possible American space station. The two "wings" are solar panels which use the Sun's rays to make electricity.

Moon probes

All kinds of unmanned spacecraft have been used to study the Moon, land on it and explore it.

Russian spacecraft of the Luna series orbited the Moon, landed on it and sent back soil samples. The American programme included Lunar Orbiter and Surveyor spacecraft that explored possible landing sites.

△ An astronaut on the Apollo 12 mission to the Moon inspects the spacecraft Surveyor 3. The Apollo 12 Lunar Module landed only 180 m (200 yards) from the unmanned Surveyor Moon probe, which had landed $2\frac{1}{2}$ years earlier.

The Apollo astronauts took some Surveyor parts back to Earth.

Probes to the planets

◁ The picture shows the unmanned Russian spacecraft Luna 17 (above) about to land on the Moon.

After landing, ramps were unfolded (below). The vehicle that rolled down the ramp was Lunokhod 1, looking like a bathtub on wheels. It was steered from Earth.

▽ The Voyager space probe. Two of these were launched in 1977 to study the distant planets.

Only unmanned space probes have been sent to study the planets. Manned missions may follow in the future.

Probes to Mars, Venus and Mercury – the closest planets – have sent back information and photographs. Pioneer and Voyager probes have explored the outer planets. They have returned remarkable pictures of Jupiter and Saturn and their moons.

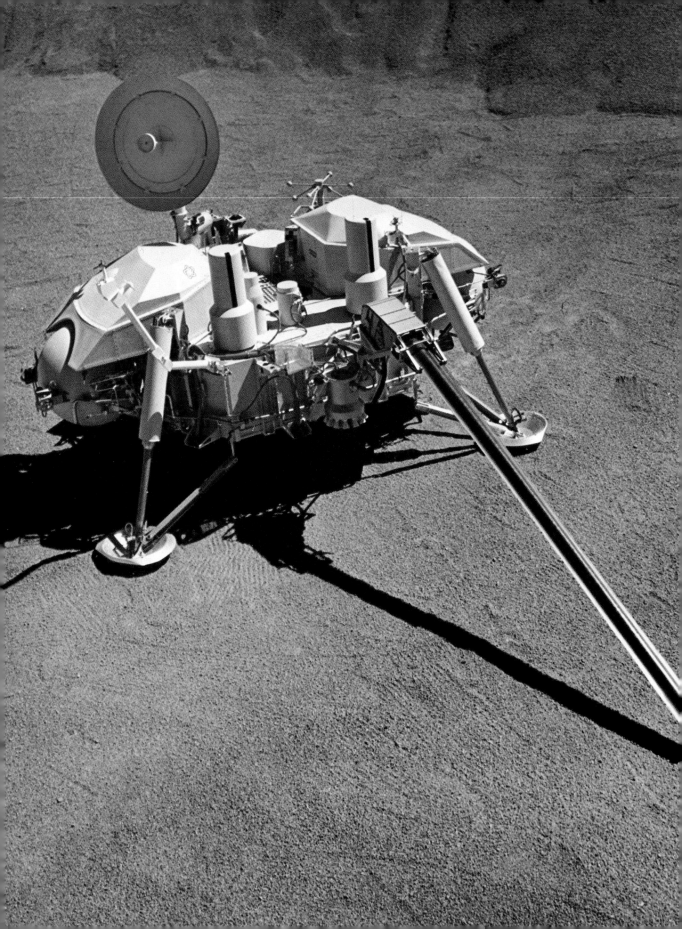

◁ The Viking Lander scooped up Martian soil to test for forms of life. It did not discover any.

Viking made many other studies on Mars. It examined the landscape with TV cameras and it also recorded wind, temperature and other weather measurements.

▽ The Pioneer 10 spacecraft was the first probe to pass Jupiter.

Planetary probes travel in orbits around the Sun. Some fly past a planet. Their instruments are so sensitive that they can measure a planet's temperature from tens of thousands of kilometres away.

Some probes are sent into orbit around a planet, or even to land on it. The Viking Lander on Mars tested the planet's soil for signs of life.

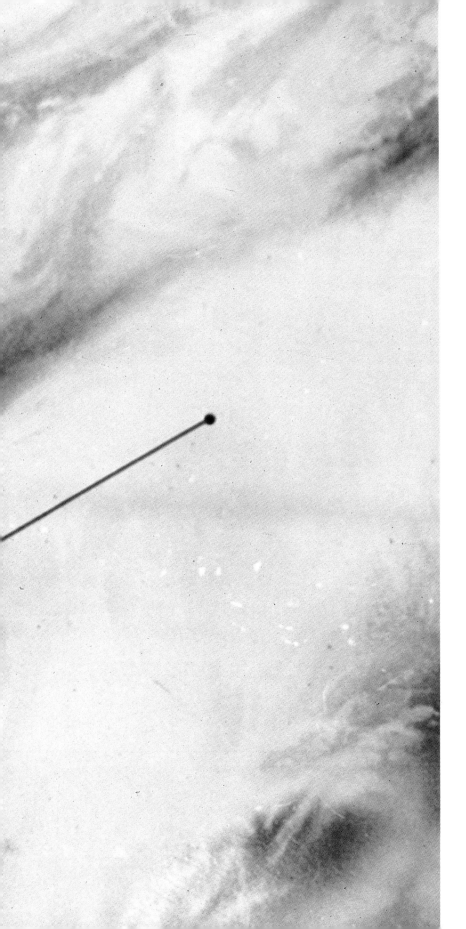

◁ The picture, painted by an artist, shows Pioneer 10 as it flew past Jupiter. It passed within about 130,000 km (81,000 miles) of the giant planet.

Controllers used over 200 different commands to operate Pioneer 10. It took four days to pass Jupiter, and commands took 45 minutes to reach it.

Pioneer sent back a great amount of information and pictures of Jupiter. It carried on far beyond the planet on its way to becoming the first spacecraft to leave the Solar System.

Rocket launchers

Spacecraft are launched by a whole range of rockets. The heavier the spacecraft, the more powerful the rocket has to be.

Launch vehicles are built up from a few basic rockets, which operate in stages. Powerful first, or booster, stages include Atlas and Titan rockets. The Space Shuttle system uses two solid-fuel booster rockets.

▷ Mercury 4 lifts off atop an Atlas rocket.

▽ The giant rocket Saturn V leaves the Vehicle Assembly Building at Cape Kennedy with Apollo 11 on the crawler-transporter. The three-stage Saturn V rocket, topped by the Apollo spacecraft, stood 111 m (363 ft) tall.

The story of spacecraft

Rocket power

A rocket works by sending out a stream of hot gas from a narrow nozzle. This has the effect of propelling the rocket in the other direction.

The secret of launching a spacecraft is to provide enough rocket power to enable it to overcome the pull of Earth's gravity.

First steps in space

It is thought that the Chinese invented the rocket over 1,000

△ Explorer 1 made the first scientific discovery in space, a belt of radiation.

years ago. In the late 1800s, the Russian rocket pioneer Konstantin Tsiolkovsky worked out how it would be possible to send rockets into space by using stacks or clusters of rockets. Near the end of World War II the Germans used rockets to send bombs to Britain. After the German surrender, their leading rocket expert Wernher von Braun went to the US to pioneer the American space programme.

It was the Russians, however, who started the Space Age,

△ One of the early Sputnik spacecraft.

when they launched Sputnik I on October 4, 1957. A month later they sent a dog into space in Sputnik II. The US joined the "space race" on January 31, 1958, when they launched Explorer I.

The space race

The rivalry between the US and the USSR continued.

Spacecraft of the Russian Luna series flew past the Moon, crash-landed on the Moon and

△ The official emblem of the Apollo–Soyuz link-up in space.

△ Gemini 6 and 7 made the first rendezvous in space, in 1965.

took pictures of its far side, all in 1959. In 1960, the US launched weather, navigation and communications satellites.

In 1961, the USSR launched the first manned spacecraft, and Yuri Gagarin became the first man in space. In the mid-1960s, US spacecraft achieved the first

rendezvous and docking in space, and in 1969 landed the first men on the Moon. In the late 1970s, the European Space Agency began launching satellites.

With more satellites, planetary probes, space stations and Space Shuttle, our use and exploration of space goes forward.

△ A European Ariane rocket ready to launch a satellite.

Facts and records

Space emergencies

It is remarkable how few mishaps and accidents there have been with spacecraft. A spacecraft has many thousands of parts and systems where things can go wrong. In manned spaceflight, there have always been many risks.

Tragedy struck in 1967, when three American astronauts and a Russian cosmonaut lost their lives in accidents. In 1971 another three cosmonauts were killed in space.

△ The Russian Luna 10 spacecraft, which became the first satellite of the Moon, in 1966.

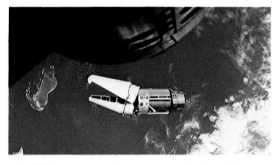

△ Things went wrong with the Agena target vehicle after the first space docking and Gemini 8 (top) had to make an emergency return to Earth.

Other disasters have been avoided by the skills of the astronauts and ground control. The astronauts of Gemini 8 had to make an emergency return and landing when the docking with an unmanned Agena went wrong. In 1970 the Apollo 13 mission had to be abandoned when an oxygen tank exploded on the way to the Moon. The crew returned safely to Earth.

Another emergency was launch damage to Skylab, which was successfully repaired by Apollo astronauts.

Slingshot in space

Mission planners of probes to the planets are able to use the gravitational force of a planet to slow down or speed up a probe. In this way, for example, the Voyager spacecraft were "hurled" from the orbit of Jupiter onward to Saturn just like a slingshot in space.

Glossary

Booster rocket
An additional rocket or rocket stage used to boost the speed of a spacecraft.

Dock
To join up with another spacecraft in space.

Lunar Module
The part of the Apollo spacecraft that landed on the Moon.

Orbiter
The spacecraft part of the Space Shuttle system. It orbits the Earth.

Payload
The cargo of any launch vehicle, usually a satellite.

Probe
A spacecraft sent away from Earth to explore space and anything in it, such as the planets.

Rendezvous
To meet another spacecraft in space.

Salyut
A series of Russian spacecraft used as space stations.

Satellite
Any body that orbits another body in space. Orbiting spacecraft are artificial, or man-made, satellites.

Skylab
The orbiting laboratory that made solar and other studies in the 1970s.

Solar panel
An array of solar cells that convert the Sun's rays into electricity for running a satellite or other spacecraft.

Solar System
The Sun, the planets and everything within their orbits.

Space Shuttle
The re-usable spacecraft that returns to Earth and lands like a plane after each mission.

Space station
A spacecraft that remains in orbit and is serviced by other spacecraft, which bring changes of crew.

Spacelab
A laboratory that is taken up in the cargo bay of a Space Shuttle.

Index